INVOKING THE SPIRITS

THE OCCULT INFLUENCES IN
EZRA POUND'S PISAN CANTOS

KATRINA MAKKOUK

TRAPART

INVOKING THE SPIRITS

Trapart Books 2024

ISBN 978-91-988711-9-7 (Paperback)
ISBN 978-91-988711-7-3 (E-book)

Copyright © 2024 Katrina Makkouk

Trapart Books / Carl Abrahamsson
Storgatan 3, SE-598 37 Vimmerby
Sweden

info@trapart.net
www.trapart.net

TABLE OF CONTENTS

FOREWORD

This project began as an investigation into the modernist ideals of poetry. "Make it new" is both a rallying cry and motto for much of the modernist poetry movement which echoed for decades after Pound's original conception to drag the Victorian era writers, poets, and creatives fully into the next century. Poetry for the sake of art met its match in Ezra Pound. His unfailing charge towards change is what sets apart his work from many other writers and poets. He embraced an idea and did not let it go despite popular opinion or political climate.

This text is an examination of Pound's time spent briefly with W.B.Yeats and others during his London years. What follows is an investigation into the echoes of this period in London that haunted Pound's memories in the distressing and life-changing time he spent incarcerated in Pisa during World War II.

As much of this text follows an original thesis project, credit must be given to the authors whose works are cited here. Without the research, facts, and analyses of Carl Abrahamsson, Walter Baumann, Ronald Bush, Richard Ellmann, Leon Surette, and Demetres Tryphonopulous, this expanded investigation into *The Pisan Cantos* would not have been possible. These foundational studies set the stage for this investigation of Pound's metamorphosis from young poet to epic master whose *Cantos* are a much valued cornerstone of modernist literature.

Thanks must be sent to Carl Abrahamsson and Vanessa Sinclair. Their encouragement and support enabled this thesis idea to morph into a little book shared amongst friends and scholars alike whose projects have led into the world of magic and mystical practices. An open mind and dialogue can unite believers and skeptics alike to see that there is great value in studying and sharing what is unknown, strange, or frightening. Magic offers a place of refuge for everyday practitioners as well as scholars. It is my hope that this book will encourage others to bravely step beyond the veil of the ordinary to seek the mystery and magic beyond.

CHAPTER ONE

OCCULT INITIATION: POUND AND W.B. YEATS

Despite being written some thirty years later, *The Pisan Cantos* are in part a product of the occult education Ezra Pound received in London between 1909 and 1916. One of the most influential occult figures in Pound's developing occultism was W.B. Yeats. During the Stone Cottage winters between 1913 and 1916, Pound served as secretary for Yeats and often accompanied him to various occultist meetings in London. Despite his fierce admiration for his mentor, Pound approached occult study and experimentation with a fair amount of reserve for what did not seem to him an altogether practical pursuit. Nevertheless, because of his exposure to Yeats and the London occultists, Pound's writing shows obvious occult characteristics such as his inherent exclusivity, personalized form of automatic writing, and invocation of the dead.

Under Yeats's guidance, Pound's academic pursuit of occultism influenced his writing and became a theme to which he often returned. Chapter One establishes the connection between Pound's London years, the occult education he received there, and the occult characteristics that begin to manifest in his poems. Pound found a use for his belief in the "aristocracy of the arts" through the occultist teachings of exclusivity and sharing of select knowledge. This chapter introduces Pound's use of *The Odyssey* as a method for reinterpreting his occultism through séances and the spirit world. Chapter Two focuses on Pound's development of automatic writing in his poetry and how it is the primary method of composition for his much later *Pisan Cantos*. Chapter Three analyzes Pound's occultism by focusing on the séances, ghosts, and demons present with *The Pisan Cantos*. By proving that occultism is a primary factor within Pound's writing, I am contributing to the scholarship initiated by Leon Surette and Demetres Tryphonopoulos. This thesis will prove how Pound's occultism is a valuable tool for understanding his poetry and that his occultism should not be ignored as an uncomfortable academic subject.

Occult study has the regrettable problem of bestowing a sense of eccentricity to any author affiliated with it. Today's acceptance of all things mystical or magical, whether it be witchcraft, spells, crystals, or seances, has morphed into a cultural touchpoint–a zeitgeist. In popular culture, the notable Satanic Panic of the 1980's gave rise to the idea that occultism had a causal relation to deviancy and other sinful behaviors. This caused many occultists, witches, and even casual practitioners of the magical arts to go "underground" as the risk of being shunned or persecuted for non-traditional beliefs clashed with the cultural turn towards conservatism. This panic was simply a follow up act to an avoidance of magic and all things occult for many hundreds of years. However, culture wars are the very foundation upon which radical ideas are born, and encountering a general fear of the unknown combined and dealing with mainstream opinions was nothing new to poets such as W.B. Yeats and Ezra Pound. Together, they changed the course of modern literature. Modernist writers and poets opened the door for investigations of the occult variety to be an acceptable practice rather than one hidden behind closed doors.

This leads to the necessary task of defining, "What is occultism?" In general, the definition of occultism encompasses the practice of magic for the purpose of gaining supernatural insight. For a scholarly interpretation, Demetres Tryphonopoulos defines the term, "...to mean the whole body of speculative, heterodox religious thought which lies outside all religious orthodoxies. As well, occultism involves the belief in the possibility of gnosis or direct awareness of the Divine" ("Occult Education" 74).

Occultism today has evolved into an even more personal practice. For example, the practice of witchcraft or spellwork can provide the practitioner with a way to gain insight into the supernatural such as seeking guidance for one's personal life choices. A tarot reading or séance can connect us with higher meaning, purpose, and can provide clarity during uncertain times or challenging trials. The practice of magical arts is rooted in mystery, but is worth exploring through an academic or scientific lens to gain knowledge and a new perspective.

Leon Surette discusses this issue in his indispensable book *The Birth of Modernism*. He writes "Like Pound's fascism, Yeats's occultism has been a subject not to be raised in polite company" (9). Surette attributes the lack of scholarly interest in studying modern occultism as an academic subject to its stigma of being taboo and misconstrued. Polite company plays by the rules of society. The rigid-backed approach to poetry was exactly what Pound sought to change as he believed the Victorians to be firmly stuck in the past. Yeats, however, was engrossed in his study of the occult and was willing to drag polite society with him into its depth. Under his guidance, seances became an arguably fashionable trend in wealthy drawing rooms rather than something to be seen as evil and corruptive. Occultism to Yeats was simply another path for him to delve into in his research as he strove for a way to touch the supernatural. Yeats's lifelong interest in occult study gave him connections between his strong sense of spiritualism, Irish nationalism, and religious upbringing.

After establishing his friendship with Yeats, Pound began to develop his own interest in the occult through a less romantic perspective than his mentor, preferring a more academic point of view. Pound cultivated his occult ideas based upon what Tryphonopoulos calls the "celestial tradition." This celestial tradition combines the pursuit of supernatural wisdom with the mythology of the ancient classics. The works of Dante, Homer, and other canonical writers provide Pound with recurring themes in his epic *Cantos* as well as his *Pisans*. This proves his involvement with the occult movement in London is a largely unaccredited influence in his *Cantos*. By employing the occult as a tool for scholarship rather than a zeitgeist in modern literature, the negative connotations it carries can be dispelled.

Fascination with the occult had swept quickly across the literary landscape of Europe prior to Pound's 1908 arrival in London, where Yeats had already become an established practitioner of the occult. Yeats's curiosity about magic and all manner of occult subjects led him to join Madame Blavatsky's Theosophical Society in 1897. The group's central doctrines were built around "...Eastern religions, from European occultism, mysticism, philosophy, and when it served their purpose, from science" (Ellmann 62). As a theosophist, Yeats became head of the Esoteric Section which studied, "secret symbols, themes between parts of the body, the seasons, the colours, elements, and the like" (Ellmann 67). When his committee failed to produce a single magical result despite Yeats's enthusiastic experimentation and research, he resigned and promptly joined the Hermetic Order of the Golden Dawn. Yeats hoped to continue his esoteric studies with support from the Golden Dawn. Ever unsatisfied with his work, Yeats became determined to find a method to combine his literary interests with the supernatural knowledge he so desperately sought. In his biography *Yeats: The Man and the Masks*, Richard Ellmann discusses how the poet's occultism advanced so that it became a firmly established presence in his life and impacted nearly all his literary endeavors. Ellmann's perspective is that Yeats's goal "was to mould both occultism and nationalism into his art" (118). His innate desire to maintain exclusivity in his work found fulfillment within the Golden Dawn's stringent levels of authority and rituals of initiation required to access occult secrets. The rituals Yeats took part in as a member of the Golden Dawn led to "visions" which are described by Ellmann as "symbolic meditations." The visions are a precursor to Yeats's attempts at automatic writing. These meditations were meant for mediums to use "their imaginations to dwell on ancient divinities, who would often obligingly seem to take definite shape and to enlighten them on various aspects of the other world" (126). As a result of these visions Yeats began to keep a diary for his occult studies, testament to the level of sincerity with which he approached these practices. His continued research and experimentation only solidified his belief in the possibility of gaining knowledge from the spirits. Yeats's search for supernatural wisdom and enlightenment were well advanced by the time Pound attempted to make the acquaintance of the respected elder poet.

Being initiated into Yeats's exclusive inner circle brought Pound a step closer to achieving his goal of modernizing poetry. In Pound's opinion, Yeats possessed the talent and connections he needed to introduce new life into the old and unfashionable modes of Victorian poetry. Pound made his rounds through meetings such as the Poet's Club and the Irish Literary Society in an effort to establish himself as one of London's literati and claim a much desired invitation to Yeats's Monday Evenings. This meeting is where the most exclusive group of poets gathered at Yeats's behest (Longenbach 11-12). After gaining an invitation to join this elite circle of artists and writers Pound still felt as if he had not yet reached his full potential. Inspired by Yeats's earlier Rhymer's Club, Pound organized his own exclusive two man group which he dubbed the Order of the Brothers Minor. The two-member group, consisting of only himself and Yeats, significantly raised his status as one of London's newly distinguished modern poets.

Despite having minted a friendship with Yeats, Pound did not begin his mentorship immediately. After his acceptance of Yeats's offer for a secretarial role at Stone Cottage, Pound wrote to his mother in dismay that he was afraid his time with Yeats would not be profitable due to the elder poet's ongoing investigations into psychic research ("Occult Education" 77). Yeats's fascination with the supernatural did not coincide with what Pound deemed necessary study for modernizing poetry. In an effort to please Yeats, Pound initially assumed the role of "interested and informed outsider." Even though he attended "many gatherings of people interested in esoteric matters held by Yeats and his occult friends Pound did not see himself, nor was he seen by them, as belonging" ("Occult Education" 77). Nevertheless, Pound went to occult meetings with an open mind and concentrated on finding ideas to share with Yeats such as his theories on symbolism and aesthetics.

As Yeats's involvement with the occult became more dedicated, his Monday Evenings developed into mostly a gathering of his closest occult associates including G.R.S. Mead, A.R. Orage, Allen Upward, the Shakespears, and Laurence Binyon. These meetings spanned all the major occult groups such as the Theosophical Society, the Golden Dawn, the Quest Society, and minor groups whose roots grew from the Freemasons and the Rosicrucians. After Yeats introduced Pound to this diverse set of occultists, the young poet began his occult education. Occultism gave Pound the resources and vision to bring a fresh perspective to modern poetry.

Although much of Pound's early career was spent amongst these occult groups, Tryphonopoulos correctly points out that Pound's occultism is largely overlooked by scholars and widely undervalued as a theme in his poetry. He argues that Pound's occult education and subsequent plans for an epic poem began well before his first meeting with Yeats. He notes that Pound's interest in the occult began in 1904 due to his relationship with concert pianist Katherine Heyman. Tryphonopoulos writes that Pound's feelings for Heyman inspired him to read occult literature as a way to share her interests. Heyman is known to have interpreted music through an occult perspective and voraciously pursued her own occult education (*Celestial Tradition* 63). Tryphonopoulos's argument stands in opposition to Longenbach's, whose *Stone Cottage* is dedicated to the assumption that the most important initiator for Pound's occult education was Yeats. There is not sufficient evidence to say conclusively that Heyman initiated Pound into the occult before Yeats although there is little doubt that she had a strong influence over the young poet. She must also be credited by aiding Pound in his quest to meet Yeats after moving to London. I am inclined to take Longenbach's position that Yeats was Pound's primary occult teacher. Tryphonopoulos argues that Pound's time spent with Miss Heyman produced only a minor interest in "fashionable occult literature" (*Celestial Tradition* 65). Pound's budding occultism began to thrive after he had been exposed to Yeats's research and occult acquaintances.

Pound favored his occult connections because of the exclusivity these groups created amongst themselves. Tryphonopoulos introduces the idea that it is Pound's "elitist attitude" rather than the "thematic correspondence" that encouraged his attendance at occult meetings ("Occult Education" 81). Longenbach's perspective closely mirrors my own that Pound's goal was to create a superior form of poetry to energize traditional Victorian composition. After his acceptance to London's "occult milieu," Pound developed an enduring interest in myth and initiation rituals. These subjects quickly became recurring themes within his poetry. In an effort to please Yeats and challenge himself with new subject matter, Pound became involved with publishing his article submissions to G.R.S. Mead's magazine *The Quest*. Tryphonopoulos outlines the relationship between Pound and Mead as one of teacher-student and that Pound's admiration for Mead was founded upon scholarship and his well-rounded occult knowledge ("Occult Education" 82).

One of the primary arguments for Pound's occultism emphasizes his voluntary article submissions for Mead's magazine. Pound's friendship with Mead fostered other important occult contacts, including Allen Upward. Pound was introduced to Upward at one of Mead's Quest meetings in 1911 and they quickly became friends and colleagues. Both men shared a scholarly approach to developing literary theories and a similar attitude concerning occultism. Upward was one of the more skeptical participants in Yeats's ongoing psychic experiments. When Pound was introduced to Yeats in May 1909, Yeats had already made significant progress in his occult research. At the time, he was most involved in a study of practical magic in the form of theurgy (*Celestial Tradition* 76). Pound's initial perceptions of Yeats's occultism were founded on his sometimes unconventional experiments and their results. For the literary community in London, occultism aided in the development of modernism. Because of a correlation to literature and art, studies of the occult began to transform into more serious scholarly pursuits rather than a vogue pastime. Pound's many collaborations with his colleagues provide a strong argument for his occultism through the evidence of his literary contributions to occult scholarship.

Pound succeeded in linking his occult and non-occult interests by fostering an attitude of exclusivity created with Yeats through their mutual desire to modernize literature. James Longenbach devotes a major point in his book *Stone Cottage* to discussion of Yeats and Pound's preference for maintaining exclusivity within their work in order to attain more authority within London's literary scene. Longenbach attributes their bond to a shared "impulse to insult the world" with harsh criticism and similar arrogant attitudes. Pound's arrogance resulted from having Yeats as one of his primary influences (73). Yeats understood his pupil to be a fiery poet and brash young man not unlike himself during his days as political activist and haughty Irish nationalist. Within the Order of the Brothers Minor, Yeats's voice was more dignified and experienced, which caused a bit of tension with his protégé at times (Longenbach 71). Pound's need to promote exclusivity within his work gave him a certain amount of dominance over his literary peers despite his inexperience and youth. He gleaned this approach from Yeats, whose desire for exclusivity in his work found fulfillment within the Golden Dawn's rites of initiation and levels of authority which granted access to occult secrets. The brief examination of the occult groups discussed here offers a glimpse into how difficult it may have been for Pound to access occult secrets despite his close association with Yeats. After undergoing his own initiation, Pound adopted the occultist method of sharing select or secret knowledge as a tool for exclusivity to compose his poetry. Pound's understanding of occult exclusivity and select knowledge originate from an interest in historicism based on his readings of Dante, Homer, and tomes of the classic philosophers. These studies supplied Pound a natural accompaniment to Yeats's occultism. Pound discovered, as Surette writes, that the occult shares with literary modernism "an interest in philosophy of history, in secret history, and in the history of religion and mythology" (*Birth of Modernism* 23).

By combining myth, history, and secret knowledge in his writing, Pound constructs an environment of initiation into which he can bring his readers. He believed that gaining comprehensive understanding of a people or culture resulted directly from the initiation of the reader. Pound's *Cantos* are notoriously full of bits and pieces of news, language, and references which the average reader might find challenging. Pound initially defended his choice of difficult material and the lack of understanding amongst his readers by saying, "YOU WILL NEVER KNOW either why I chose them, or why they were worth choosing, or why you approve or disapprove my choice, until you go to the TEXTS, the originals" (*ABC of Reading* 45). In his poems, Pound recreated the occult perspective that once a reader is initiated, then true understanding of the material will follow.

I agree with Surette's perspective on this point that "Pound's message is *echt*[1] occult. Surette writes that this occult teaching is represented throughout the entirety of *The Cantos*; meaning hidden through obscurity of surface is typical Pound. In effect, "*The Cantos* are intended only for initiates, or perhaps more accurately, for those whom the poem itself can initiate into the mysteries it obscurely manifests" (Surette 35). I agree with Surette's argument that Pound's writing is less "mystical visionary," but instead follows a more Blakean tradition. Pound's visions are not meant to be shared with the everyman. As Pound learned from Yeats's occult friends, new members must pass

------

1 Definition: genuine or authentic

initiation rituals before they can be privy to even the lowest level of occult secrets. Pound used this elitism in his poems as a means to maintain an air of authority reminiscent of his London years. Pound intended for his poems to provide illumination for the unenlightened. In layman's terms this sometimes makes Pound's poetry seem as if it is at best a complex mix of citations. This "obscurity of surface" is not unfamiliar to his other work, including his *Guide to Kulchur*. Surette heralds the text as "a cranky book" even for Pound wherein he continually suggests there is a secret "too profound to be plainly uttered" (Surette 100). Surette's argument concerning these texts builds upon the idea that Pound's work contains ambiguous occult historiography inclusive of the secret history of Europe, America, and China (37). By hinting at these secret histories or select knowledge, Pound can be identified as the initiator just as Yeats was his initiator into the occult.

During the Stone Cottage years, Pound expanded his role as an initiator by working both as Yeats's secretary, his occasional editor, and radical modernist. Pound's exclusive attitude, use of language, and attention to unfamiliar references gave him authority to impart or restrain select knowledge just as he had learned from his occult peers. Pound stood by his opinion that to be enlightened one must be well read. In *ABC of Reading* Pound writes "It is my firm conviction that a man can learn more about poetry by really knowing and examining a few of the best poems than by meandering about among a great many" (43). Even the most comprehensive study of Pound's classics would still not yield to the average reader full disclosure of his secret histories and myth so as to make his poems more approachable. Lee Lady offers the metaphor that "Reading the *Cantos* is like paying a visit to a wonderful enormous shop run by a devoted antiquarian....He walks you around the shop and shows you all sorts of unusual objects...to the shopkeeper, each of these objects has profound significance, and as he shows them to you he expects you to be able to appreciate this significance" ("Reading Ezra Pound's *Cantos*"). Pound's writing is permeated by his Odysseus obsession and dedication to what Longenbach defines as the aristocracy of the arts. Pound used this basis of select knowledge to establish the foundation of his epic cycle of poems, *The Cantos*.

Pound's motivation for writing *The Cantos* originated from his occult education and use of secret history, initiation, and invocation of the dead. Tryphonopoulos and Surette both agree that Pound's *Cantos* are supposed to be read as an initiation for the reader into the world of culture and myth. This point of view directly opposes the argument that *The Cantos* is simply an extended journey taken by Pound's secondary Odyssean mask. Surette notes that *The Cantos* are better understood through an occult approach. He writes, "The dead who appear in *The Cantos* are wise rulers, great artists, and a few villains. *The Pisan Cantos* are much more like a séance for they are dominated by Pound's recollection of friends—both dead and absent..." (124-125). Pound combined his occultism with his intention to write an "epic 'including' history." Surette's discussion of Pound's historical epic as a practice in occult séance admittedly does not conclusively provide a cohesive element to *The Cantos*, but does provide an answer for the foundation on which *The Cantos* are built. This makes the readability of the text in its entirety a study in occult initiation, Pound's personal reflections, and inclusive of historical narrative.

In his article concerning Pound's occultism, Tryphonopoulos does not delve into the difficulty of reading Pound's historicism alongside the Homeric themes prevalent throughout *The Cantos*. Pound's exclusive attitude and occultism is attached to his reading of Homer's *The Odyssey* and Odysseus's journey through the world of historic myth. The figure of Odysseus becomes the embodiment of Pound's idealism and politics which are inseparable from his occultism. Surette writes that "Pound's poem would reveal the pattern hidden in the steel dust of historical events" (125). In his later *Cantos*, Pound attempted to amalgamate his occult interest in the "secret history of Europe," keeping personal record of unfolding historical events, and in his darkest hours summoning the dead in his Pisan séance.

The argument concerning whether Pound's *Pisan Cantos* are more autobiographical than his earlier *Cantos* is irrevocably linked to Pound's occultism and political ideology. This line of questioning comes as a result of his perceived fascist sympathy and support for Mussolini's regime. Although his sentiments carry overtones of fascist propaganda, Pound's desire to continue his epic *Cantos* and establish a legacy is the pivotal point of *The Pisan Cantos*. Pound's "séance" brings back the ghosts not only of fallen fascist leaders, but of friends and mentors as well. He remembers the ghosts of his past while continuing the séance he began with Yeats during his London years. Canto 76 finds him considering a reference to his occult education:

> spiriti questi? personae?
>
> tangibility by no means *atasal*
>
> but the crystal can be weighed in the hand
>
> formal and passing within the sphere... (76.217-220)[2]

---

2 All references to Ezra Pound's Cantos follow the text of *The Cantos of Ezra Pound* and are cited by Canto number and line number.

Interspersed throughout this canto are references to the "crystal" or sphere. For a student of the occult, the practice of using crystals for spiritual healing or guiding energy is commonplace. There is the double entendre of occult reference for the crystal and the sphere of heaven which he could glimpse through his "smoke hole" (76.288). The spirits surrounding him in the passage are questioned by Pound. He is caught in a tangible plane of being and cannot grasp "Union with the Divine." Pound's struggle between two planes of existence are a consequence of his confines at the American Disciplinary Training Center and the mental duress of his imprisonment. The longer he is in the little cage the more he seems surrounded by ghosts from his past. Pound himself seems caught in his own invocation of "Death/ insanity/suicide degeneration" as he suffers beneath the burden of not knowing who of his friends have survived the war (76.154). He decides that:

> nothing matters but the quality
> of the affection—
> in the end—that has carved the trace in the mind
> dove sta memoria" (76.157-160)

The memories that haunt him throughout the *Pisans* are woven together by his images of ghosts and gods. In his introduction, Richard Sieburth describes *The Pisan Cantos* as "a séance during which the poet takes dictation from all various voices and personae that have been summoned to inscribe themselves on the palimpsestic writing pad (Freud's *Wunderblock*) of his psyche" (*Pisans* xxiv).

Just as *The Pisan Cantos* are designed to fit into the larger schema of *The Cantos* epic, Pound's occult initiation ritual for his audience continues from one canto to the next. Tryphonopoulos writes of *The Cantos* that "The obscure and hermetic nature of the poem embodies the initiation for the reader" in an attempt to create "an actual revelation or mystical experience" (*Celestial Tradition* 62). In the *Pisans* Pound returns to his theme from Canto I where Odysseus is faced with a descent to the underworld. Tryphonopoulos discusses the important use of the classical epic tradition of a hero who will descend to the underworld or *nekuia* where after battle he will come to enlightenment or *gnosis*. In Pound's English translation of Andreas Divus's Latin translation of *The Odyssey* for Canto I, he uses Odysseus' descent and journey towards *gnosis* which is symbolic of Pound's own *katabasis*[3] as he writes his own epic. Pound acknowledges that his version of the reinterpreted Homer is indebted to the Divus edition. Pound

---

3 Descent; particularly a descent to the underworld.

commands the ghost of the translator, "Lie quiet Divus. I mean, that is Andreas Divus" (1.68). By pointedly mentioning Divus's name, Pound felt some disagreement with the prior version preferring to take the text and translate it personally. By completing a new translation of the Divus text, Pound built the foundation of an occult initiation ritual. Tryphonopoulos suggests "...that, motivated by his familiarity with Hellenistic ritual, Pound reads the ancient works as representation of initiation rituals having a common origin" (*Celestial Tradition* 103). The ritual sacrifice Odysseus performs for Tiresius brings forth:

> Dark blood flowed in the fosse,
> Souls out of Erebus, cadaverous dead, of brides
> Of youths and at the old who had borne much;
> Souls stained with recent tears, girls tender,
> Men many, mauled with bronze lance heads,
> Battle spoil, bearing yet dreory arms,
> These many crowded about me; with shouting,
> (Canto 1.28-34)

The goal of Odysseus's sacrifices in this canto is to gain access to the world of the dead—an intangible plane where Pound's Odysseus will eventually attain *atasal* or Union with the Divine. The souls he conjures as a result of the ritual are a part of a "spiritualistic séance or necromancy" (*Celestial Tradition* 105). Divus and the ghosts of Odysseus's dead men are the first ghosts filling the expansive mausoleum of *The Cantos*. The spirits crowd around Pound and follow him throughout *The Cantos* as he reaches towards enlightenment. Whether he ever has the "magic moment" as Tryphonopoulos calls it, is an unanswered question. Even in his later *Pisan Cantos* Pound seeks *gnosis* and the promise of Paradise in the DTC amongst his ghosts and goddesses.

As he continues his initiation ritual and Odyssean journey in *The Pisan Cantos*, Pound uses a form of automatic script to describe his visions and séance. This re-emphasizes the influence of his occult education and legacy of his relationship with Yeats during his London years. In the *nekuia* at the American Disciplinary Training Center, Pound was in the unique position of writing what he perceived to be a final set of poems. Since fear of death and uncertainty consumed Pound, he turned to a type of automatic script in which to house his calling forth of ghosts, spirits, and gods to witness his perdition as an American traitor and disgraced poet.

CHAPTER TWO

POUND'S AUTOMATIC WRITING IN THE PISAN CANTOS

Pound began writing his *Cantos* in 1915 while under Yeats's mentorship in London, and the long poem spans over more than five decades.There are more than one hundred and twenty completed poems aside from the numerous revisions and drafts. The myriad of subject matter in *The Cantos* includes historical and current events, Pound's ongoing autobiography, political revelations, and at least six languages. Before World War II, Pound was working on the section known as his Italian *Cantos*. These poems are written in Italian and approach propagandistic material. From 1940 to 1943, Pound had a bi-weekly radio broadcast supporting Mussolini's regime. Deemed an American traitor, Pound was arrested in 1945 and sent to the American Disciplinary Training Center in Pisa. While incarcerated Pound composed ten poems published as *The Pisan Cantos* in 1948. His next section of *The Cantos* was written during his thirteen year internment at St. Elizabeths Hospital. These cantos, published as *The Rock-Drill* and *Thrones*, are followed by the final chapter of the epic *Drafts and Fragments of Cantos CX–CXVII*. After he was released from on grounds that he would not stand trial, Pound moved back to Italy. His final set of cantos was published in 1969.

There is no surprise that his formative years as a poet would be the most influential for Pound's development of *The Cantos*. Inspired by his occult education, Pound becomes the initiator while writing *The Cantos*. His primary motivation is his belief that readers must be cultured. As established in Chapter One, Pound's initiation ritual begins with a re-telling of Odysseus's journey to the underworld where battles his way back home to Ithaca. Pound returned to the *nekuia* theme and his Odyssean masks as a guide for continuing his epic *Cantos* when he was imprisoned from May to November 1945 at the American Detention Center. Pound's "poem including history" applies not only the occult teachings of initiation and exclusivity, but also employs automatic writing as the method of composition. My analysis of *The Pisan Cantos* reveals that Pound's unique form of automatic writing is evident through his visions, secondary personality, spirit guides, and invocation of the dead.

For automatic writing to occur, the medium or writer must be receptive to creative and supernatural influences. In an automatic writing session, the primary goal of the medium is to produce writing inspired by supernatural or spiritual influence. Automatic writing can assume several formats including free-hand drawings, abbreviated phrases, and even multi-lingual composition. *The Online American Heritage Dictionary* defines automatic writing to be, "Writing performed without conscious thought or deliberation, typically by means of spontaneous free association or as a medium for spirits or psychic forces." The primary objective is to discern a subconscious or spiritual meaning from thought processes not always fully understood or accessible to the writer. A more experienced writer can serve as a medium for the spirits. Ellmann summarizes automatic writing as "... chiefly a matter of suspending conscious use of the faculties" (225). Traditionally automatic writing emphasizes a shared "ancestral memory" which is one source for the select knowledge the spirits may share in a session (Nally 58).

During his London years, Pound became familiar with occult experimentation including automatic writing, its connection to the medium's identity, and autobiographical nature. On more than one occasion he witnessed Yeats and his fellow occultists hold séances and practice automatic writing for the purpose of divination or prophesy. Several of George and W.B.'s first automatic writing sessions were undertaken at Stone Cottage. After nearly six years of automatic writing sessions with his wife, Yeats published their results and his theories concerning esoteric thought in *A Vision*. The perspective of many self-proclaimed occultists concerning automatic writing is that the practice is more parlor trick than serious research. Even amongst occult circles Yeats was sometimes regarded as having a peculiar obsession with the occult. In *The Birth of Modernism*, Surette points out that many writers in the modernist clique tried to disassociate themselves directly with occult activities. He writes "Pound, Joyce, and Eliot are all on the record with disparaging remarks about Yeats's ghosts." (12). Despite the cold reception to all things magical and mystical, Yeats and his closest occult associates engrossed themselves in automatic writing and its sister activity, the séance, in their quest for divine knowledge.

Yeats firmly believed that "life carries on in the spirit world" which "emphasizes that the spirit is never value neutral, and always seeks to sustain or reinforce the beliefs of the sitter and/or the medium" (Nally 58). As Yeats grew more experienced in occult experiments, he desired a more personal way to communicate with the spirit world in addition to regular séances and other psychic tests. He dedicated himself to automatic writing for the purpose of "charting the odyssey of the Soul" (Harper "Unbelievers" 4). The need to gain access to the spiritual realm drove Yeats to seek communication with the spirits by assisting his wife, George, who became a medium during their automatic writing sessions. Their results are documented in what became Yeats's *A Vision*. Yeats's earlier studies had produced *Per Amica Silentia Lunae* written as a summary of Yeats's belief in the after-life, the role of a daimon, and encounters with the spirit of Leo Africanus. In *The Wisdom of Two*, Margaret Mills Harper gives insight to the details of the Yeats's occultism and their writing of *A Vision*. In their pursuit of automatic writing, Yeats and George explored how the mind can be used as a powerful tool for channeling the spirits. Harper discusses an essay Yeats wrote to attempt to define the myriad of occult and religious beliefs pervading his poems and plays:

> The topic of faith in this essay then acts as W.B.Y's other occult prose does, as an enchantment, best to a rhythm of sound and rhetoric reminiscent of spoken ritual or oral rhetoric, syncopated by a tome that vacillates between assertion and imaginative contrarily, and bracketed by social and political contexts that do not define the subject, as culture might be expected to do, but rather are used by that subject. (*Wisdom of Two* 62)

Yeats, his wife, and even Pound gave their study of the occult a sense of academic purpose. Although Pound did not embrace his occult education as a fully religious experience, Yeats was able to make connections between his faith and occult studies.

At Stone Cottage Pound generally held himself aloof from many of Yeats's occult practices since he had dedicated his attention to the Fenollosa papers, but he gained familiarity with its purpose as Yeats grew more deeply involved in his studies. Ellmann discusses one of Yeats's ongoing tests with automatic writing which took him more than two years to complete, beginning in 1912. In this experiment, Yeats endeavored to ask questions by method of telepathic communication and have them answered by one of his automatic writing participants. He became unfailingly convinced that "a living mind could serve as a medium for departed spirits" (198). This test is among many that Yeats conducted while sharing a close association with Pound in London. Although Pound never became fully ingrained in the occult as his mentor did, he found value in retaining elements from his occult education in his *Cantos*. Pound remembers his Stone Cottage studies in *The Pisan Cantos* when he thinks of "Uncle William / downstairs composing" (83.165-166). He writes regretfully:

> well those days are gone forever
> and the travelling rug with the coon-skin tabs
> and his hearing nearly all Wordsworth
> for the sake of his conscience but
> preferring Ennemosor on Witches (83.184-188)

As Yeats's secretary, Pound's duties included reading aloud to the elder poet. There is little surprise that Yeats preferred Ennemoser's text over the Romantic Wordsworth. Ennemoser's book includes investigation into animal magnetism and occult science, which would have been a primer for Yeats and Pound who were "scientifically illiterate" (Surette 150). The occult sciences were an aside to Yeats's progression in psychical research which Ellmann writes was a product of Yeats's quest to find "irrefutable evidence of the supernatural" (196). Pound took an interest in reading those occult texts alongside Yeats and developed a more latent occultism which was exposed in his *Cantos*.

The occult education Pound underwent more than thirty years prior to his imprisonment in 1945 is an important factor in his composition of *The Pisan Cantos*. The occult overtones of the *Pisans* are generally ignored in favor of discussing Pound's politics and autobiography. In a reflection of his first canto, *The Pisan Cantos* are written as Pound's "nox animae magna" where he is both Odysseus descending to Hades and "no-man" (74.431). James Longenbach addresses the underlying question as to other motivations for composing *The Pisan Cantos*. He writes, "The *Pisan Cantos* are Pound's autobiography, his own genealogy of the dream of nobility." His legacy is inherently tied to Yeats since, "Even when Yeats is not mentioned in *The Pisan Cantos* (and he does appear more often than any other ghost) the presence of his sensibility is always felt" (Longenbach 175). Pound lists the ghosts whose presence he is aware of including:

> Fordie that wrote of giants
> and William who dreamed of nobility
> and Jim the comedian singing...
> (74.69-71)

He notes in this passage what Sieburth calls the "shades" of Ford Madox Ford, W.B. Yeats, James Joyce, Victor Plarr, Edgar Jepson, Maurice Hewlett, and Sir Henry Newbolt. These men are all part of Pound's "aristocracy of the arts" that lived on well past his London years. This aligns with Surette's opinion that modernism and occultism both share the elitist approach, acceptance of secret histories, and pursuit of wisdom within their respective canons (122-123). He writes, "Yeats, Orage, Upward, Mead, and Weston all endorsed the theosophical story of ineffable wisdom surviving from great antiquity" (123). Pound wrote *The Cantos* based upon secret history while weaving *The Odyssey* into its fabric to complete the formula for his epic. Yeats once said that Pound's epic ambition was "'constantly interrupted, broken, twisted into nothing by its direct opposite, nervous obsession nightmare, stammering confusion...'" (Longenbach 172). Yeats's analysis of Pound's work offers a deeper understanding of the poet who has relinquished himself to become a medium for his ghosts and the dream of an epic legacy within the *Pisans*.

Sieburth's introduction to *The Pisan Cantos* presents the idea that because Canto I is based upon Book 11 of *The Odyssey*, Pound wanted his epic to take a similar journey "back into origins, sacrificing blood to give voice to the shades of the heroic past." He points out that, "the anamnesia enacted by the *Pisans* is far more internalized or subjective, turning as it does on the poet's free-associational excavation of the various buried strata of his own personal past..." (Sieburth xxviii). Pound wrote under the pressures of war and possible death as he channeled his inner thoughts, as if this set of cantos would be read as his final broadcast set to paper. Through mental and physical duress, Pound sets forth to create a poem which he knew might be his last opportunity to derive meaning from the war which had gained him an unwelcome position as the celebrity prisoner of the DTC. The fact that Pound wrote earlier drafts of *The Pisan Cantos* series does not prohibit the argument that the poems he wrote while imprisoned are a product of his unique style of automatic writing and mediumship. Sieburth writes that "the sheer velocity at which Pound's pencil riffs down the page nonetheless points to a compositional technique rather different than the one which had informed his previous Cantos." (Sieburth xxiv). He gives himself up in mediumship as he channels his epic through the realm of myth.

The ghosts who haunt *The Pisan Cantos* guide Pound from the road to hell and onto the path towards a meditative close as the poet becomes possessed by the Odyssean spirit as he believes death is imminent. He begins Canto 80 with an adamant plea against his imprisonment as he channels the conversation of his fellow inmates:

> Ain' committed no federal crime,
> jes a slight misdemeanor" (80.1-2)

Pound never apologizes for his controversial stance concerning fascism and carried this loyalty with him through *The Pisan Cantos* and into his stay at St. Elizabeths after his release from the DTC. His indignance at the war and his forced silence in the DTC is evident in his derision of all things American from politics to dialect. Pound's later incarceration at St. Elizabeths only solidifies his love and admiration for Italy, its language, and sometimes misguided government. The inmates surrounding Pound in the DTC creates a distaste for America's brand of justice as he sat alongside serious criminals; his only crime having exercised his freedom of speech. He reminisces about his peers and old literary theories in an attempt to retain his composure in the unforgiving environment of the DTC.

From this point onward the canto carries Pound's "death-chill" (80.33) into automatic script conjuring the ghost of friends and colleagues who:

> ...as Santayana has said:
> They just died   They died because they
> just couldn't stand it (80.86-87)

George Santayana is quoted here because Pound must have been familiar with his theories concerning metaphysical naturalism and may have possibly read his *Realms of Being*. In addition to Santayana's cultural significance which Pound's initiated readers would understand, Pound reflects on his shared acquaintance with several of Santayana's students such as T.S. Eliot and Gertrude Stein. His concerns about solidarity and epic legacy undermine his ability to peacefully accept his own death which leads him from death to resurrection theories. He considers Thomas Beddoes and his theory of resurrection after death based upon the bone *luz* as well as the partial resurrections of corpses during Cairo's all souls day (80.160-169). The idea of resurrection is only briefly entertained before he admits to approaching the end of his wits at "the gates of death" (80.660-661). With no hope of escape from mental and physical duress, Pound allows the Odyssean spirit and his occultism to emerge as sources of strength and inspiration.

Pound's use of his Odyssean ego is a conscious application of a developed secondary personality. I will use the terms "personality" and "mask" interchangeably here because of their varying interpretations in Poundian scholarship. Most studies of automatic writing I've researched support the possibility of a secondary personality as a type of shield for the medium's hidden emotions. As mentioned in Chapter One, mask theory functions in an almost identical manner by allowing the author to escape duress or persecution through the protection of a mask.

From an academic or scientific perspective, automatic writing is more than just a tool to contact the spirits or to gain supernatural knowledge and guidance such as Yeats and his wife did. In her scientific exploration of automatic writing Dr. Anita Muhl finds that the practice does not have to be a mysterious or curious endeavor. Muhl's work as a psychoanalyst led her to study the practice of automatic writing as a therapeutic tool, and she published her findings in her 1930 book of the same title. The perception upheld by Muhl is that automatic writing can be utilized as a way to clear the mind; the practice is influenced by the writer's personality, experiences, and memories.[1] In opposition to Muhl's scientific use of automatic writing is the perception that it may be practiced by a mentally unstable individual. In *An Encyclopaedia of Occultism*, Lewis Spence says that automatic writing can be produced as a result of "a slight disturbance in the nerve centres occasioned by excitement or fatigue to hystero-epilepsy or actual insanity" (56). Spence's analysis of automatic writing as a symptom of fatigue is applicable to Pound as he suffers through imprisonment. Spence's explanation is an example of Tryphonopolous's argument that the study of the occult is widely viewed as a superstitious and disreputable activity. Spence's stance assumes that only mental or emotional instability would influence someone to undertake automatic writing. I agree with Muhl's argument because based on her research automatic writing can actually combat and heal emotional stress by providing the medium an outlet for expression. Muhl's argument offers a much more charitable explanation for the belief that Pound must have suffered from insanity and his emotionally charged Pisan poems are the result.

In my efforts to understand automatic writing, I created a project built on the idea that automatic writing can be used in the therapeutic sense to support my argument that Pound uses automatic writing in his Pisans. Pound's fusion of therapy and the writing of poetry is intriguing. I asked ten people to follow the basic rules Muhl outlines in her text to identify the purpose behind practicing automatic writing. The participants were asked to sit quietly for ten to twenty minutes, clear their minds, and simply write or draw what they felt. Summarily, all the participants said they felt a sense of emotional release from stress. Several of the results included pictures, phrases, and nonsensical sentences one participant said was the inspiration for a new story he

---

1 This argument is upheld by Anita Muhl in her exposition on automatic writing. However, I'd like to note that despite many non-scholarly texts and websites available for automatic writing research, there is a general lack of academic sources aside from individually published articles on the subject.

intended to write. The effect of automatic writing is difficult to execute for those who were self-described as "stressed out" and "too tired to think." Overall the clinical applications of Muhl's automatic writing analysis proves to be applicable to Pound's situation as he sat under the burden of emotion caused by his imprisonment. As I discovered as a result of my project, automatic writing takes a great deal of silence and concentration to be used effectively. This supports my argument for Pound's use of automatic writing since the results of my exercise are remarkably similar to Pound's method of composition for *The Pisan Cantos.*

Muhl's analysis of automatic writing as a form of therapy also reveals that developing a secondary personality, or as Ellmann calls them, "masks," is a common development amongst mediums. For many automatic writers, the secondary personalities revealed in their sessions are connected to their formative years and do not have to be linked to a mental imbalance or a spirit guide per se. This is evident by how the Pound-Odysseus character in the *Pisans* wanders freely between Pound's memoir and a mythical Homeric landscape. In Canto 82, Pound combines his translation of Aeschylus's *Agamemnon* with a roll call of figures whose presence were important in Pound's past. He introduces the scene reference to Agamemnon's murder and a watchman standing by, "On the Atriedes roof"/ "like a dog...and a good job" and (82.23-28). He pauses the Agamemnon story to recount several important figures: John Masefield, Stanislawa Tomczyk, and Richard Reithmuller among others. I argue that Pound's recollection of a renowned medium, Miss Tomczyzk, is proof of how important his occult education was to his work.

> Miss Tomczyk, the medium
> baffling society for metaphyscial research
> and the idea that CONversation.....
> should not utterly wither (82.52-55)

In keeping with Muhl's perspective, it is evident how Pound's automatic writing as a therapeutic tool helps him retain the memories he so feared to lose. The peculiar method of combining myth with his past suggests that Pound finds value in maintaining a balance between biography and mask. Pound's use of memory and myth in Canto 82 is a tool to deal with the stresses of the prison environment. In addition to promoting secondary personalities, automatic writing is useful in revealing a writer's previous experiences in a safe and therapeutic manner.

Pound's contribution to the scholarly argument surrounding

occultism is based largely on how he approaches the practice of automatic writing. It is his adamant opinions about the necessary changes required to modernize literature and art that makes his poetry the foundation for modernism. Aside from the obvious experimental aspects to composing in automatic script, Pound is a proponent for making literature and poetry "new" by employing different techniques and theories. As will be discussed in Chapter Three, Pound's theory of the occultist birth and death cycle, *palingenesis*, is directly connected to his use of automatic writing. He takes a traditional occult practice and reinvents it as a method for composing poetry. While writing *The Pisan Cantos* Pound uses automatic writing as a therapeutic tool for channeling a séance. The seemingly nonsensical jumble of subjects in the *Pisans* assume a more coherent structure when viewed through the lens of automatism.

Automatic writing can function as a way to dispel personal fears since the act of automatic writing is the tool for releasing emotional energy. Spence writes, "As a rule automatic speech and writing display nothing more than a revivification of faded mental imagery, thoughts, conjectures, and impressions which never come to birth in the upper consciousness" (56). With this method a writer can access hidden feelings or memories which give an autobiographical or narrative focus to their sessions. In her analysis of automatic writing from a medical academic perspective, Muhl explains some of its uses:

> In obtaining quickly the subject's own explanation of delusions, fears, obsessions, and hallucinations. As a means of bringing phantasy into actual expression. As a means of recalling forgotten incidents. To explain and elaborate other visual imagery. (38)

Pound's automatic writing enables him to come to terms with his fears and state of exhaustion. Physically and emotionally fatigued, Pound scrambles to write another chapter for his epic and to support his brief attempt at an autobiography. Pound drafts his poems as quickly as he can in an effort to preserve his memories. He applies the emotional distress from his imprisonment to create a set of poems so unique with his automatic writing style that they were given the Bollingen Prize for poetry after his release from the DTC.

As we see in *The Pisan Cantos*, Pound continually invokes the aid of several spirit guides in the form of gods and ghosts as a method of coping with his demons in the DTC. In Canto 76, Pound sees:

> But on the high cliff Alcmene,
> Dryas, Hamadryas ac Heliades
> flowered branch and sleeve moving
> Dirce Ixotta e che fu chiata Primavera
> in the timeless air (76.6-10)

The unfamiliar surroundings of the DTC put Pound in a morbid and rapidly disintegrating state of mind. He seeks hope and solace in the figures of the nymphs and muses from his view of hell provide him comfort. The muses, Dirce, Isotta, and Giovanna are symbols to Pound to grasp as he feels helpless amongst the "cages" of the DTC. These women and the figures of nymphs and ghosts become Pound's guardians throughout the *Pisans*. As Ronald Bush discusses in his article, the "suave eyes" watching Pound belong to otherworldly female figures in a passive but protective manner (189). Through the filter of a séance, Pound is calling forth spirits who can aid him in his passage through hell.

Bush notes how just before his imprisonment Pound's writing reflected the political turmoil in Italy. After being taken to the DTC, Pound begins keeping a "diary-like notebook" of his thoughts. At first he "laments a world in ruins and seeks consolation in a landscape suffused with Greek and Confucian presences" (171). These presences are a few of the spirit guides we encounter throughout Pound's Pisan journey. His ever increasing fear of memory loss and death leads him to hold a séance of ghosts and continual "testimonials to the dead" (197). His séance is filled with friends who have passed away and Pound looks to them for hope of his much sought-after Paradiso. By attempting to retain his memories, Pound's mnemonic exercise becomes "like a mantra that sidesteps physic resistance and discovers sympathetic powers beyond the ego" (197). Pound imagines seeing guiding goddesses:

> "With us there is no deceit"
> said the moon nymph   immacolata
> give back my cloak, *hagaromo.*
> had I the clouds of heaven
> as the nautile born ashore
> in their holocaust
> as wisteria floating shoreward
> (80.260-266)

Taken from one of Pound's earlier Noh plays, *hagaromo* refers to the cloak lost by an "aerial spirit" or the moon nymph (Sieburth 146). Pound also sees Venus as born ashore perhaps in reference to Pound's longing for the safety of home and the love of a woman. These female apparitions appear indirectly too when Pound's encounters "suave eyes, quiet not scornful." Although the figures that possess these eyes vary between each canto, Pound navigates the landscape of his poem under their gaze. Bush writes, "the suave eyes then initiate a poem whose theme involves the redeeming energies of light and reason." Where they belong to Aphrodite in Canto 80 with "pale eyes without fire," then the more subtle eyes Pound sees in Canto 81 (189-190). Pound immerses himself in his visions of Paradise, aware of the eyes watching over him. These goddesses Pound sees throughout the *Pisans* are similar to Yeats's experiences during their Stone Cottage years. As Pound learned from his occult education, one objective for an automatic writing session is to reveal supernatural visions outside of the medium's physical reality. Pound believes in Paradise but questions:

> I don't know how humanity stands it
> with a painted paradise at the end of it
> without a painted paradise at the end of it
> the dwarf morning-glory twines round the grass blade
> magna NOX animae with Barabbas and 2 thieves beside me,
> the wards like a slave ship,
> (74.389-394)

Within a few weeks of his imprisonment, Pound loses his hope of freedom and his thoughts turn towards the possibility of death. In these lines he falters between faith in the "painted paradise" beyond his prison walls and the damnation of hell. His vision of heaven becomes connected to his loss of freedom in the DTC. At one moment he can see Paradise and then as it slips away he searches in vain for something to renew his faith. Pound places himself in the role of the crucified Jesus experiencing his soul's darkest hour. He employs the symbolism of a savior put to death for the sins of others to represent his feelings of betrayal at his detainment. Over the course of *The Pisan Cantos* it is Pound's sense of loss and unfulfilled faith that brings him to an emotional breaking point. As he searches for solace in the midst of his *nekuia*, Pound resumes the occult speculation of the afterlife and its connection to humanity. Pound's automatic writing is driven by the ghosts and spirits he raises throughout his Pisan séance.

Another primary component for automatic writing is the personality and identity of the writer. Pound uses these characters as masks to portray himself under the shroud of a mythical hero—Odysseus. Pound became familiar with invoking a mask to cover personal shortcomings or feelings when he lived and worked alongside Yeats. Ellmann argues that the poet needed a way to resolve his internal conflicts (199). Yeats uses his masks as a protective shield from rejection and insecurity. He also sought to bring forth the spirits of the dead through the masks of his daimons. Pound's ideal mask is the illusion of a hidden hero. In his study of mask theory in his book *Ezra Pound and the Pisan Cantos*, Anthony Woodward posits that Pound is fully absorbed into the use of masks and they take over his performances in *The Cantos*. Woodward writes, "In the *Pisan Cantos* the poet's own self, having been largely absorbed into mask, pastiche, and translation in earlier *Cantos*, for the first time appears on stage—a histrionic image that comes naturally to the pen and has its odd appropriateness" (12). In contrast with Woodward's argument for Pound's complete absorption in the masks of his characters, I argue for the use of masks as a tool for automatism. To summon a large number of characters from varying histories and traditions to the stage of his *Cantos* Pound needs a method for easy transition making the mask tool particularly effective. Odysseus, as Pound's stronger personality, shoulders the duress of imprisonment and carries Pound through the *Pisans* as a victorious warrior instead of a disheartened poet. Pound develops his hero-identity through Odysseus and uses this mask regularly throughout the *Cantos*. These many sides of himself which come together in the chaos of his *Pisans* are similar to the struggle Yeats endured with the self and anti-self. Ellmann's biography of Yeats posits that this concept of anti-self is the driving force behind Yeats's use of masks within his work. Ellmann writes that Yeats's mask is a construction of the poet's social self which cannot merge self-perception with how the world perceives him (175-176). For the purpose of writing his epic, Pound crafts his own Odyssean mask and occult "Higher Self."

From the first canto in the *Pisans*, Pound identifies himself through his Odyssean personality. In *The Pisan Cantos*, his Odyssean character fulfills the dual role of mask and spirit guide for Pound's automatic writing. He identifies:

> OU TIS, OU TIS? Odysseus
> the name of my family (74.23-24)

The Greek translation Sieburth offers is "no man," which is the name Odysseus adopts to trick the Cyclops (Pound, *Pisan Cantos* 120). This merging of personalities consistently reappears throughout the *Pisans* as Pound's defense against his journey through the hell of the DTC. He reasserts again in Canto 74:

> in telling the tales of Odysseus   OU TIS
>   OU TIS
> "I am noman, my name is noman"
> but Wanjina is, shall we say, Ouan Jin
> or the man with an education
> and whose mouth was removed by his father
>   because he said too many *things* (74.61-67)

Sieburth's notes discuss the fact that tales of *The Odyssey* were similar to those told of the prophet Elijah. In a further blurring between his Higher Self and Odysseus, Pound imagines himself to be both a prophet and a reincarnation of the creator of the world, Wondjina, also called "man of letters." Just as the creator-god has his mouth removed, Pound shares this similarity with the enforced silence of his imprisonment during the first few weeks in the DTC. By composing his *Pisans* via automatic writing Pound regains the control he lost through use of his radio broadcast and then the enforced silence of his jail cell. Pound begins to see himself as:

> OU TIS
> A man on whom the sun has gone down
> Nor shall diamond die in the avalanche
>   Be it torn from its setting
> First must destroy himself ere others destroy him. (74.192-196)

In these lines, Pound writes from the perspective of Odysseus, who is battle-weary and far from home. Pound shares with Odysseus a feeling of diaspora. Pound's feeling of displacement shares similarities with Homer's hero whose idealism and resolve is unwavering despite his situation. By continually reasserting his Odyssean personality, Pound creates a guide who navigates the difficult terrain of his *Pisans*. Pound learned from Yeats that to successfully integrate oneself into automatic writing it is necessary to have a spirit guide. Pound puts his Odyssean mask as his guide "ere others destroy him." I would like to suggest that Pound naturally uses Odysseus in his automatism because the Homeric spirit had already been with him in his cantos and in his poet's mind for many years.

    As his life seems past hope and his imprisonment wears on him, Pound calls forth ghosts and spirits in a séance meant to help him preserve his memories. Throughout the *Pisans* Pound constantly encounters the world of the dead. In the depths of his *nekuia,* Pound communes with ghosts in the séance he hosts in *The Pisan Cantos.* For six months, Pound tries to find his Paradiso and allows the "suave-eyed goddesses" to guide him there. Pound's occultism reaches its climax as he conducts a séance that his automatic writing calls forth.

CHAPTER THREE

"DRIVE OUT THE DEMONS": POUND'S PALINGENETIC CYCLE

When examining *The Cantos* as an entire body of work it is evident that Pound never relinquishes many of the influences of his early years. An analysis of *The Pisan Cantos*, written some thirty years after his first draft of *Three Cantos*, reveals that Pound's occultism, interpretation of cultural history, and passionate political views are themes saturating his entire epic. As Walter Baumann aptly writes, "*The Cantos* is so full of details which are at first sight utterly incoherent that it has been called a rag-bag" (15). As a result of this "rag-bag," the structural and linguistic chaos of *The Cantos* finds resolution through Pound's intention to write poems utilizing the occult education of his youth. As discussed in Chapter One, Pound's occult education extensively influences his use of initiation rituals and exclusivity in his writing. Chapter Two examines Pound's method of composition for *The Pisan Cantos* as a personalized form of automatic writing. Within this chapter I will prove Pound's occultism through his use of palingenesis and séances in *The Pisan Cantos.*

The belief in initiation through palingenesis, a symbolic death and rebirth into an enlightened state of being, is a remarkably copied motif within the occult societies of Pound's London years. As noted in the first chapter of this thesis, initiation rituals are the primary methods to test new members for their readiness in receiving access to exclusive occult knowledge. When Pound met Yeats in 1909, the elder poet's desire to share his occultism with his new protégé resulted in Pound's introduction to rites of initiation and the ideology of rebirth and enlightenment. Yeats underwent initiation rituals several times, most notably with the Golden Dawn and the Theosophical Society (Ellmann 89-101). Ellmann summarizes the necessity of this process noting that, "Secret societies are usually divided up into two parts; when the initiate has passed through the first part he has so purified, so trained his faculties that his earlier self is said to die. Now he centers on a new life..." (91). Joining an occult group as an initiate requires being open to the possibility of supernatural powers and an elevated plane of being through palingenesis (Surette 119). Yeats and Pound share the idealism of attaining a higher plane of existence although with decidedly different goals. Yeats's ambition to prove how the supernatural touches everyday life is evident by his documented research. Pound's "higher plane" focuses on attaining a new perspective with art, literature, and his modernist and political theories. The similarities between the two poets' understandings of an enlightened state of mind are shared through their belief in the afterlife and the purpose of the birth-death cycle. Pound uses this idea in his poetry to combine the Homeric *nekuia* with his modern "epic ambition."

Hugh Kenner's *The Pound Era* acknowledges Pound's ability to reach beyond reality to the "higher plane." Kenner argues that *The Pisan Cantos* contain "an invasion of the great dead, to speak through him [Pound] and receive his signature on their cadences" (486). Pound's *Cantos* are ripe with the words of long-dead and dying men and women whose influence over Pound extends past their graves. Pound makes his poems a bridge between life and death just like one of Yeats's séances. This connection between Pound's occult education and the appearance of ghosts in his cantos is a remarkably ignored theme in his work. The premise of Pound's séance not only exists to call forth the dead but also to highlight his theories concerning palingenesis. His occult education taught him that the way to gain to be reborn must be to figuratively "drive out the demons" to make a place for the enlightened mind of an initiate. Kenner and Surette argue that Pound makes his *Pisans* both a séance for communing with the dead while himself being reborn. I propose adding discussion of Pound's interest in history to Kenner and Surette's point of view. I argue that Pound's cyclical perspective on history is directly connected to his occult perspective regarding palingenesis. Pound's experience with the devastation of two global wars gives him the unique point of view that war, death, and birth are irrevocably connected to the afterlife. At Stone Cottage Pound is only an observer to the passing regiments of soldiers. His disapproval of the politics motivating World War I is echoed through *The Cantos*. He considers war an unnecessary bi-product of political waste. This distaste turns to grief as Pound mourns friends lost to both sides of the war. This solidifies his need to call forth the dead via séance throughout *The Cantos*. Friends and loved ones are dead, but not forever gone. The occult palingenetic cycle gives Pound the promise of enlightenment through death.

Pound is drawn towards the descent to hell in *The Odyssey* because it symbolizes his own personal journey between the war and his séance for the dead. This is one of the primary purposes of the *nekuia* in *The Pisan Cantos*. Surette writes that Pound's Odyssean theme of descent and subsequent communication with the dead is itself a palingenetic motif (115). In his first canto, Pound aligns himself and Odysseus with the idea that enlightenment must be born from death. This thought is identifiable in his much later *Pisans* as he considers the impact of the war. Pound says in Canto 77:

> With drawn sword as at Nemi
>   day comes after day
> and the liars on the quai at Siracusa
>   still vie with Odysseus
> seven words to a bomb
> dum capitolium scandet
>   the rest is explodable (77.95-101)

 The Latin references *Ode III* by Horace translated as "I shall arise with fresh praise in the future, as long as the High Priest climbs the Capitoline Hill with silent virgins" (Sieburth 146). Pound begins this passage with a reference to the sacred Lake Nemi where Diana's temple stood guarded by a priest who is murdered by another jealous of his position. Horace calls Diana the "three-form goddess" as she is thought to represent the goddess of the underworld, a huntress, and goddess of the moon. Diana is also symbol of fertility and childbirth. Her juxtaposition with the atomic bomb exploding on Hiroshima brings the image of the cycle of birth and death. Pound's point in this passage is to reveal the unforgiving ferocity of the cycle of destruction and death; he focuses on how man can be enlightened through learning from history. Pound understands history to be itself palingenetic but irrevocably caught in a cycle of death. Similar to the stories of Odysseus told again and again, Pound watches war repeat itself with no knowledge as to how to stop the process. Pound views himself as trapped in a vulnerable state of being where his beloved Italy, his memories, and life are at stake. He is haunted by the memories whose solidity is slipping away. He considers the emotional pain of the people and places he loves destroyed by a useless war. In his journey to rebirth, Pound steps toward the "timeless air over the sea-cliffs" seeking freedom from hell (76.92).

The motif Pound uses over and over again throughout *The Pisan Cantos* is the image of a precipice in contrast to the *nekuia*. Pound views his detainment in the DTC as the symbolic death of his old life and searches for glimpses of Paradise beyond his cell walls. He draws from the Homeric perspective of the underworld in contrast with the image of the ocean and a barrage of waves mercilessly pounding the shore. The image of the sea in the *Pisans* becomes muddled between his Odyssean story and the pool of his memories. He writes in Canto 83:

>   A fat moon rises lop-sided over the mountain
>   The eyes, this time my world.
>   But pass and look *from* mine
>   between my lids
>   sea, sky, pool
>   alternate
>   pool, sky, sea, (80.196-202)

Longenbach sees in this passage the comparison of Pound's imprisonment in the DTC and his altercation with police at Stone Cottage so many years before Pisa. Although I do not share the same perspective as Longenbach, his analysis of the importance of Pound's memories is applicable to the argument in this chapter. Longenbach writes, "The memory of this event, a symbolic end to the noble dream of the Brothers Minor, must have been especially charged for Pound.... Authorities had come for him the second time, and there was no one left to write to" (263). In this passage Pound becomes as one of his spirits in the Pisan séance, present yet without the ability to influence change. In contrast to Longenbach, Ellmann argues that Pound's use of the elements is linked to his memories and his ongoing séance. In these lines there is Pound's point of view from his mind's eye of the moon literally in the landscape of his mind's eye. Ellmann argues that the *Pisans* fit elementally into earth, air, water, and light. The importance of these elements is how they work with Pound's other motifs. Throughout the *Pisans*, Pound grasps tightly to his memories and calls upon the dead in an attempt to stay the onslaught of waves assaulting his memory. Ellmann eloquently writes that it is Pound's memory which brings "strange phantasms into the dusty place" (476). Fading like a ghost, Pound begins to use the séance as a method for dealing with his varying emotions. By freeing his mind of its emotional burden Pound succeeds in establishing a recurrent séance in the *Pisans*.

As discussed in Chapter Two, Anita Muhl's analysis of automatic writing argues for its indispensable use as emotional therapy. As Sieburth notes in his introduction, the process of writing *The Pisan Cantos* becomes a séance "during which the poet takes dictation from all the various voices and personae that have been summoned..." to Pound's consciousness (Sieburth xxiv). Under the watchful eye of his "suave eyed" goddesses, Pound hosts conversations with spirits of the dead. These personae join Pound in his descent to hell as he becomes another "noman" no-name prisoner "with an education" (74.63-65). He removes the cloak of self-importance he assumes during his Radio Rome broadcasts and finds himself alone with his hero-identity in shambles. Similar to Odysseus's search for redemption and home, Pound's journey through the world of death and decay puts him onto the path of enlightenment towards heaven.

In his examination of Pound's *Cantos*, Leon Surette argues that Pound's Paradiso is obtainable by undergoing a palingenetic initiation. According to Surette, visiting the underworld like "Orpheus, Odysseus, Lazarus, Dante, and the questing knight—are in truth exoteric representations of palingenetic initiation" (106). Pound perceives his *nekuia* through the perspective of one who seeks the guidance of the dead to reach gnosis. I agree with Surette's argument that Pound's palingenesis must go through the death stage and as a result *The Cantos* and his *Pisans* are filled with a "summoning of the dead." The problem in classifying Pound's writing as a séance is that his *Cantos* do not follow a specific pattern or chronological order. This presents an issue for identifying ongoing themes and motifs since Pound can briefly write about one subject and without transition begin speaking of something entirely unrelated. There is an overall difficulty in arguing for a consistent séance in Pound's writing except that it is, as Surette argues, "the only embracing structural principle possessed by this enormous poem" (125). There are other structural theories to be considered other than a séance of course. Walter Baumann's examination of Pound's writing generally lends a historical connection between the poems. This is not incorrect, but I argue that it is Pound's use of cyclical history combined with the rebirth idea which gives the *Pisans* a connection to his other *Cantos*. Pound questions his mortality and turns to his ghosts to aid him in his search for Paradise. In *The Pisan Cantos* Pound continually wonders:

> we recall him
> > and who's dead, and who isn't
> > and will the world ever take up its course again?
> very confidentially I ask you: Will it? (76.36-39)

His poem is rooted in the uncertainty of the death and irreparable damage caused by the war. He remembers World War I and the impact it has on him personally as well as his writing. Sequestered at Stone Cottage, Pound and Yeats heard about the goings on of the war from a considerably safe distance. However, it is this first contact with the violence and propaganda of war that propels Pound's political interests for the remainder of his life. Longenbach writes that Pound's "...fanatical interests in social and economic programs grew from his desire to save civilization..." (132). Pound views his duty as a poet and political activist to encourage the rebirth of society and culture.

Many secret societies, including Mead's Gnostics and Yeats's Theosophists, believed that séances could provide a way towards palingenesis. Pound recalls the connection between the gnostic belief in palingenesis and its connections to séances. G.R.S. Mead, one of Pound's closest occult associates, put forth the idea that esoteric tradition is responsible for the secret societies favored by modern occultists and religious faith alike. Mead's influence is even noted in *The Pisan Cantos*:

> "ghosts move about me"   "patched with histories"
>   but as Mead said: if they were,
>   *what have* they done in the interval,
>   eh, to arrive by metempsychosis at...? (74.34-36)

Although Pound's skepticism of ghost-conjuring activities such as automatic writing and séance has been pointed out, I believe that his acceptance and gradual turn to belief in the occult has been overlooked. Pound's acquaintance with Mead gave him an academic resource with which to compare Yeats's blind belief in the supernatural. Tryphonopoulos writes that Pound's exposure to Mead's Gnosticism influences him in his "conception of the 'celestial tradition,' his formulation of fantasy theory, and his theory of palingenesis or soul-making" ("Occult Education" 89). Although Mead's interpretation of palingenesis favors sexual symbolism, Pound accepts Mead's idea that wisdom can be gained through experiences which enlighten the soul. The "light from Eleusis" and wisdom of the true initiate resounds throughout Pound's writing.

In addition to the occult applications of palingenesis Pound sees similarities in Mussolini's desire for a rebirth of the Italian state and the need to initiate citizens to a better form of government. As Pound adopts Mussolini's teachings as his own, he adapts his occultist initiation ritual and exclusivity to his views of Fascism. Mussolini's own writing assumes a semi-spiritual or prophetic tone at times lending an authoritarian overtone to his manifesto. Mussolini proclaims that the Fascist state is "a higher and more powerful expression of personality" and a spiritual force (3). In *The Doctrines of Fascism*, Mussolini writes:

> Fascism...sees not only the individual but the nation and
> the country; individuals and generations bound together
> by a moral law, with common traditions and a mission
> which suppressing the instinct for life closed in a brief
> circle of pleasure, builds up a higher life, founded on duty,
> a life free from the limitations of time and space, in which
> the individual, by self-sacrifice, the renunciation of self-
> interest, by death itself, can achieve that purely spiritual
> existence in which his value as a man consists. (1-2)

One of the reasons Pound accepts Mussolini's teachings is the foundation that fascism has in the belief of a higher form of government and the goal of achieving a more divine plane of existence. This ideal resounds with Pound's earliest goal for modernist art and literature to be unrestrained by old Victorian rules by creating a society of forward thinking artists. This modernist aristocracy was Pound's way of achieving palingenesis "in the arts." In his search for connections between history, politics, and the occult Pound analyzes the key to becoming an artist who is capable of producing not only a legacy by a tool to connect to his Higher Self. In an essay written during the Stone Cottage years, "I Gather the Limbs of Osiris," Pound discusses the soul in a manner similar to Mussolini in his manifesto:

> The soul of each man is compounded in all the elements
> of the cosmos of souls, but in each soul there is some
> element which predominates, which is in some peculiar
> and intense way the quality or *virtù* of the individual; in no
> two souls is this the same. (*Selected Prose* 28)

Nearly four decades later Mussolini's own words are, "The Fascist State...stands for a principle...sinking deep down into his personality; it dwells in the heart of the man of action and of the thinker, of the artist and of the man of science: soul of the soul" (3). It is the soul of the artist and the foundations of mankind's beliefs that fascinate Pound. This is what draws him to discover more about the inner workings of the occult meetings and later what motivates him to accept the ideas Mussolini has about the principles of government. As Longenbach points out, "Pound was able to idealize the Italian state not because he extrapolated the values of a secret society of artists into a political world, but because he ultimately did the opposite" (266). In Canto 81 Pound puts forth the cry to "Pull down thy vanity" and discusses the importance of action during war:

> But to have done instead of not doing
> this is not vanity
> To have, with decency, knocked
> That a Blunt should open
> To have gathered from the air a live tradition
> or from a fine old eye the unconquered flame
> This is not vanity. (81. 166-172)

Here is a snapshot of Pound as a man of action. He adds the example that he is comparable to Wilfrid Scawen Blunt who wrote a book indicating British imperialism and was jailed for his statements (Sieburth 153). Pound shares with Blunt the feeling of being imprisoned for one's beliefs. In a politically unstable environment, both Pound and Blunt tackle countries whose ideologies stand directly against a socialist government. As a part of his "live tradition" Pound's radio broadcasts were meant to bring his ideas about Fascism to a wider audience. Although his role in the war is undefined in Canto 81, Pound does not regret his cry to "pull down the vanity" of the American appetite for war.

As Longenbach discusses in *Stone Cottage,* the political and mystical elements from Yeats's poetry directly inform Pound's attraction to the work of Sigismondo Malatesta and his adoption of Fascist beliefs later in life. Longenbach writes, "If a political leader such as Yeats's Cosimo or Pound's Malatesta provides properly for his artists, all manner of political atrocity might be excused. For Pound it was the "'state of mind'" that mattered (77). Pound sees similarities between the exclusivity of the occult search for supernatural knowledge and the Fascist idea that man should share a single guided set of principles. Both the occultists from Pound's youth and Mussolini's Fascism share the belief that in order to gain knowledge or learn from the cycle of palingenesis there must be enlightenment. As discussed in Chapter One at some length, Pound's talent gave him a natural arrogance which he channeled through the Order of the Brothers Minor and the "aristocracy of the arts." I argue that by combining his political ideas with the exclusivity and ritualism of Yeats's occult societies Pound is able to promote modernism through the lens of an occultist. Pound vehemently defends this "aristocracy of the arts" and under Yeats's tutelage ably commands some of the most influential artists in post-World War I London. Pound understands the world to be suffering from a literal and social hunger. He discusses this problem in Canto 83:

> And now the ants seem to stagger
>   as the dawn sun has trapped their shadows,
>   this breath wholly covers the mountains
>   it shines and divides
>   it nourishes by its rectitude
>   does not injury
>   overstanding the earth as it fills the nine fields
>   to heaven (83.87-94)

Pound invokes Ceres as the goddess of harvest to pointedly remark on the emptiness of war and the hunger for a better system of government. The harvest is nine fields of heaven; these fields are a symbol of early Chinese thought that there are nine levels between man and Paradise. As Pound considers the "halls of hell" there is little question as to his hope for his Paradiso beyond the confines of the DTC (81.141).

As Pound approaches the end of his *Pisan Cantos* he returns to fond memories of his time with Yeats. There is a change in this canto as Pound becomes noticeably more sentimental. The séance and demons subside as Pound seems to breathe a resigned sigh at the conclusion of the *Pisans*. Canto 83 finds Pound wandering aimlessly down the hallway of his memories. He describes "Uncle William" and his visit to Notre Dame in 1922 "in search of whatever." Yeats "paused to admire the symbol /with Notre Dame standing inside it" (83.23-27). The portrait of Yeats here is familial. Pound's attention to Yeats here denotes the importance of his role in Pound's life. Pound thinks of Yeats's ability to see past reality to the potential ethereal or supernatural symbolism within something ordinary. In contrast to his mentor, Pound nearly always saw importance in the unique and symbolism in the literal. This difference between the two poets is the element that gave their relationship balance. Pound remembers the Blunt dinner peacock which Yeats in his poem memorialized as:

> so that I recalled the noise in the chimney
>   as it were the wind in the chimney
>   but was in reality Uncle William
>   downstairs composing (83.163-166)

Even though his memories are comforting, Pound admits "well those days are gone forever" (83.184).

As Pound comes close to the final canto of his *Pisans* he looks forward to the end of his journey "Under the white clouds, cielo di Pisa" (84.70). The argument made in this thesis for the occultism evident in *The Pisan Cantos* is intended to bring more attention to, as Tryphonopoulos says, a rather overlooked portion of Pound's writing. His occultism, although admittedly not as dedicated or life-consuming as Yeats's studies, is a quintessential part of his overall tome of poems. The intertextual focus of Pound's work is exemplified in his *Pisans*.

In *The Pisan Cantos*, Pound brings a new way to filter occultism from a modernist perspective. Chapter one presents the argument that Pound's occultism is relatively ignored in favor of discussing his politics, Vorticism, and other literary theories. However, my argument throughout the course of this thesis is how the foundation of Pound's work is driven by the occult education he received in London with Yeats as his mentor. His occultism is the motivator behind his literary theories and much of his poems in *The Cantos*. Sadly, only a few scholars including Tryphonopoulos and Surette venture to claim that Pound's occultism should be studied as a central part of his *Cantos*. In such a contemporary literary age, it is unthinkable that occultism still carries such negative connotations. In Chapter One, I argue that studying literature from an occult perspective can be academic and not widely misconstrued as the interest of a few mad men. Pound views occultism as a method to bring creativity and innovation to literature. As discussed in Chapter Two, by combining his love for the classics and the role of the hero-warrior Odysseus, Pound refashions automatic writing into a useful tool for composing poetry. His earlier occult education is what gives Pound the inspiration for his séance and automatism of the *Pisans*. It is my intention that Chapter Three round out the argument for Pound's occultism by exploring its impact on his philosophical and political theories. By proving how Pound's *Pisans* are inherently an occult piece of literature, it is my hope that this study will contribute a new perspective within Poundian scholarship as pioneered by modernist occult theories.

The how and why of magic can so often be mysterious and enigmatic. For some, it does not provide entrance into an unseen world such as those sought out by Yeats. Rather, it enables the user to link themselves to the past, present, and future and to fully connect oneself to what is beyond the ordinary reality in which we find ourselves. These threads of memory and magic that are woven throughout *The Pisans* makes this set of cantos the most unique amongst the other stars of Pound's epic writing.

WORKS CITED

"Automatic Writing." Def. 1. Online American Heritage Dictionary Online. American Heritage, n.d. Web. 12 Dec. 2012. <http://americanheritage.yourdictionary.com/automatic-writing>.

Baumann, Walter. *The Rose in the Steel Dust: An Examination of the Cantos of Ezra Pound*. Coral Gables: University of Miami Press, 1970. Print.

Bush, Ronald. 'Quiet, Not Scornful'? The Composition of The Pisan Cantos." In Lawrence S. Rainey (ed). *A Poem Containing History: Textual Studies in The Cantos.*

Ellmann, Richard. *W.B. Yeats: The Man and the Masks*. New York: W.W. Norton, 1999.

Harper, George Mills. "Unbelievers In The House": Yeats's Automatic Script." *Studies in The Literary Imagination 14.1* (1981): 1. Academic Search Premier. Web. 14 Jan. 2012.

Harper, Margaret Mills. *Wisdom of Two: The Spiritual and Literary Collaboration of George and W.B. Yeats*. Oxford: Oxford UP, 2006.

Kenner, Hugh. *The Pound Era*. Berkeley: University of California Press, 1971. Print.

Lady, Lee. "Reading Ezra Pound's Cantos." Web. 10 Nov. 2010. <www2.hawaii.edu/~lady/ramblings/ABC.html>.

Longenbach, James. *Stone Cottage*. Oxford: Oxford UP, 1991.

Muhl, Anita. *Automatic Writing*. Washington: Kessinger Publishing, 2003.

Mussolini, Benito. *The Doctrines of Fascism*. New York: Howard Fertig Publisher, 2006.

Nally, Claire V. "Leo Africanus As Irishman?." *Irish Studies Review 14.1* (2006): 57-67. Academic Search Premier. Web. 14 Jan. 2012.

Pound, Ezra. *ABC of Reading*. New York: New Directions: 1960. Print.

---. *Selected Prose 1909-1965*. Ed. William Cookson. New York: New Directions: 1973. Print.

---. *The Cantos of Ezra Pound*. New York: New Directions: 1971. Print.

---. *The Pisan Cantos*. Ed. Richard Sieburth. New York: New Directions: 2003. Print.

Sieburth, Richard. Introduction. *The Pisan Cantos.* By Ezra Pound. New York: New Directions: 2003. Print.

Spence, Lewis. *Encyclopaedia of Occultism.* Mineola: Dover Publications, 2003.

Surette, Leon. *The Birth of Modernism.* Montreal: McGill-Queen's UP, 1993.

Tryphonopulos, Demetres. *The Celestial Tradition.* Ontario: Wilfrid Laurier UP, 1992.

---. "Ezra Pound's Occult Education." *Journal of Modern Literature 17.1* (1990): 73. Academic Search Premier. Web. 14 Jan. 2012.

Woodward, Anthony. *Ezra Pound and the Pisan Cantos.* London: Routledge and Kegan Paul Ltd., 1980. Print.

❧

To find other books of interest, please visit:

www.trapart.net

❧

www.ingramcontent.com/pod-product-compliance
Lightning Source LLC
La Vergne TN
LVHW092035190726
843493LV00002B/692